The People's History

Barnard Castle and the Tees Valley

by

Tom Hutchinson

Middleton-in-Teesdale School, 1925. Back, left to right: Dulcie Smedley, Nora Morton, Jenny Brown, Freda Parmley, Edna Hammill, Annie Hodgson, Winnie Bainbridge. Centre (on own) Tim Collinson. Second row: Ruth Brown, Alma Rudd, Clara Grieve, Peggy Horn, Madge Raine, Mary Corcoran, Mollie Sibson, Frances Barnett, Nancy Nixon, Ada Morton, Audrey Melench, Bertie Addison. Front includes: Leslie Bowron, Raymond Lowe, Roy Evans, ? Crabtree, Joe Baum, Claude Watson and Jeffrey Lee.

Previous page: Winston postmen ready to deliver the mail around the time of the First World War.

Front Cover: Coronation Year (of George VI and Elizabeth) 1937. Avis Charge and Joyce Allan outside the Cross Keys, Gainford in May.

Copyright © Tom Hutchinson 2002

First published in 2002 by

The People's History Ltd
Suite 1
Byron House
Seaham Grange Business Park
Seaham
Co. Durham
SR7 0PY

ISBN 1 902527 88 7

Contents

O.K. Motor Services bus AEC Regal no. AML774 at High Force Hotel on the service to Bishop Auckland. This bus was owned by O.K. from 1937-51 and the livery and fleet name details suggest a post Second World War picture, probably 1950.

HIGH FORCE HOTEL,

Forest of Teesdale, Co. Durham.

Phone: Forest 4.

The scenery of Teesdale is superb and High Force itself is the highest waterfall in England.

For botanists the area is unique; many rare and beautiful flowers being common here.

The hotel was built originally as a shooting box for the Dukes of Cleveland — King Edward VII stayed here for the grouse shooting.

It is now fully licensed and centrally heated throughout.

Produce from our own farm.

Printed and Published by F. Frith & Co., Ltd. Reigate.

TARIFF

Bed and Breakfast

17/6 Single room
32/6 Double room

Weekly Terms - 8 gns.

Lunch 5/6

Afternoon Tea 2/9 High Tea 5/6

Dinner 6/6

Tariff Card from High Force Hotel about 50 years ago.

Introduction

This book traces the River Tees from its source in Upper Teesdale to the area around its middle reaches at Piercebridge where the dale merges into lowlands and loses much of its distinctive character. It has been said that Teesdale is the most natural, complete and beautiful dale in the country. Not being a major through route means that it has been left undiscovered by the majority of travellers and tourists passing through the North East, and that, therefore, it remains unspoilt and uncommercialised.

Hopefully though, the book is more than about the river. It is about places and people from both sides of the river, the southern side of what was Yorkshire and the northern side in County Durham. It seems appropriate to divide the book into sections based on the upper river valley centred on Middleton-in-Teesdale with its agricultural and lead mining heritage; Barnard Castle, historic market town and Norman fortress; the middle Tees valley below Rokeby where the river flows through undulating countryside of corn and meadow; the area around Raby, Staindrop and Ingleton on the flanks of the watershed between the Tees and River Wear; and finally about the railway which linked the settlements in Teesdale for a century, but now is no more – along with many of the old views from early 20th century postcards.

I am well aware that books of this nature have been published before on parts of the area, so I've tried to avoid re-using pictures when inappropriate, but, of course, some views are always worth a second glance – a profile of Upper Teesdale without High Force or Barnard Castle without the County Bridge would seem incongruous – but hopefully the balance is redressed by some rare pictures. Many pictures of people appear. People make places, change the landscape. They also bring back memories and, as we get older, the memories become more important. Having said that, modern pictures of young people, in particular, also have a place – for the future.

Staindrop Girl Guides, 1982. Back, left to right: Caroline Hodgson, Joanne Gill, Andrea Douglas, Gillian Robson, Beverley Henderson, Debbie McGonagle, Lynn Carrick. Front: Christine Robson, Julie Robson, Sarah Scaife, Nicola Clasper, Lisa Walker, Joanne Waistell and Lynne Weldon.

Acknowledgements

I would like to thank and acknowledge all contributors for help, information and pictures: Beamish – The North of England Open Air Museum, Bob Abley, Stan & Betty Addison, Joyce Allan, John Askwith, Andrew Banks, Philip Battersby, Anne Bertram, Deborah Campbell, Ian S. Carr, Jim Coates, Robert Davies, Margaret Foster, Jack Gibson, Ray Goad, Mike Grantham, Charlie & Ivy Hall, John Hallimond, Cliff Howe, Brian Hutchinson, John Hutchinson, Marian Lewis, Dorothy Lincoln, Jennifer Metcalfe, George Nairn, Colin & Winnie Priestley, Parkin Raine, Kevin Richardson, Clifton Sutcliffe, Avis Tucker, Dorothy Turner, Neil Turner, Pat Stephenson, Mike Stow, Bill Swinbank, William Norman Swinbank, Alan Thornton, Ann & Peter Waistell, Geoff Waites and The Omnibus Society.

Bibliography

The Darlington Saturday Half Holiday Guide W.J. Cudworth
A Guide to Teesdale C.P. Nicholson
Barnard Castle – Historic Market Town Alan Wilkinson
Barnard Castle in Old Picture Postcards Alan Wilkinson
Around Piercebridge & Gainford in Old Picture Postcards C. & M.A. Lilley
Middleton-in-Teesdale & Neighbouring Villages Bill Payne
Teesdale in Old Photographs Dennis Coggins
Teesdale – A Second Selection in Old Photographs Parkin Raine
Backward Glances (Hutton Magna) Marian Lewis
The Life & Death of a Dales Community, Harwood-in-Teesdale J. Robinson
Kelly's Trade Directories 1906, 1925 & 1938
North Eastern Railway W.W. Tomlinson

For my Mother

A postcard of Middleton-in-Teesdale showing High Force, Kings Walk, Cauldron Snout, Winch Bridge and Jack's Scar. The card, sent from Mother at Middleton to Mrs Webster, Bracebridge, Lincoln on 30th July 1928, makes reference to 'these lovely places and all so beautiful, and very good lodgings'.

UPPER TEES VALLEY

CAULDRON SNOUT TO

LARTINGTON

Lady Rake Lead Mine, Harwood. Its total lead output, 1882-1902, was 7,106 tons, and this mine was reputed to have the highest silver content of any found in the U.K. This D.S. Sinclair, postcard publisher, card was sent from Edith at Middleton to her sister, Annie Harrison of Hawthorne Terrace, Mickleton, on 15th October 1910. By that time, lead mining had practically ceased in Upper Teesdale with the London Lead Company having been wound up in 1905 and Lady Rake being their last operating mine. However, Lady Rake was still open in 1925 according to Kelly's Directory and worked on a small scale by Lord Barnard. It had certainly closed by 1937.

CAULDRON SNOUT, Middleton-in-Teesdale.

Cauldron Snout – the largest cascade in England. The infant River Tees falls
200 feet through a long channel in the Great Whin Sill here which was once
the junction of three counties, Durham, Westmoreland and Yorkshire. This
postcard was published by George Tarn Thompson who was the postmaster at
48 Market Place, Middleton in the early 1900s. Today, above Cauldron Snout is
Cow Green reservoir by which water flow over both Cauldron Snout and High
Force is regulated.

High Force
– the
largest
waterfall in
England.
The Tees in
flood in
September,
1926, with
water
coming
down both
sides of the
dark basalt
rock and
falling 72
feet into
the deep
pool below.

High Force, September, 1926

The main fall is on the left side of the picture – which was once the Yorkshire
side – whereas the right (Durham) side may only have a slender trickle in it at
times. This card was published by J. Langstaff of Middleton who ran a
newsagent's from premises in Horsemarket

Gibson's Cave, above Newbiggin. Here water from Bow Lees Beck, a major tributary of the Tees, falls over the Summerhill fall into a deep hollow surrounded by trees. The cave is a recess behind the fall which has been eroded from the softer underlying rock so that it is possible to pass behind the descending curtain of water – though not on this date in January 1929 when the beck was frozen. The cave is said to have been named after an outlaw, Gibson, who supposedly hid in it from pursuers. Another story says it was named after a farmer who lived in Summery Hill farm nearby.

Gibson's Cave, February, 1929

WYNCH BRIDGE - MIDDLETON

Winch (or Wynch) Bridge, just below Low Force. It was put up in 1830, replacing the original one reputedly erected in 1741 by lead miners of Holwick who walked across the bridge to and from their work at Redgrove and Pikelaw mines on the fells above Newbiggin. On 20th August 1802 one of the main chains of the original bridge snapped as a party of haymakers were crossing. Two men were thrown into the water, and one, John Bainbridge of Howgill, drowned.

Holwick Shooting Box. Built by Cosmo Bonsor, M.P. in 1890 to cater for grouse shooters, though known in guide-books as 'the noble Holwick mansion.' Holwick village itself, further to the east, was the most northerly village in Yorkshire before the 1974 boundary changes which put the south bank of the Tees into County Durham. This area was and still is part of the Strathmore Estates, the late Queen Mother's family. Members of the Royal Family still visit the premises which is now called Holwick Lodge.

Heather Brae Guest House. A suitable means of transport is shown which could bring guests from Middleton about one mile below in the valley to this guest house which was built in the 1920s. The proprietor in 1938 was Thomas Rogers. This postcard sent locally from Cousin Willie and Jinnie to all at Skears. The house is now a private residence.

Wesleyan Chapel, Forest. This chapel was built in 1867 and accommodated 150 people. As in adjacent Weardale, Methodism was a tremendous force in Teesdale, and at the turn of the 20th century there was also a Methodist chapel at Ettersgill and a Baptist one at the Hagg. The chapel, known now as Forest Methodist Chapel, is closed.

Forest – A dance in aid of the hospital, 16th February 1912. Dances and processions to encourage financial donations towards hospitals – as far away as Newcastle – which served the area, were popular in the early years of the last century. This dance is being held in the local school. Forest developed as a settlement within the ancient hunting area of Teesdale Forest.

THE POSTING HOUSES, MIDDLETON-IN-TEESDALE.

Nº1087.

Middleton-in-Teesdale was first mentioned as a village connected with Staindrop and Raby about the year 1030. It is the capital of Upper Teesdale and a century ago the centre of lead mining. The two inns shown were the Blue Bell run by Matthew Coltham and the Cleveland Arms Hotel and Assembly Rooms run by William Ward. The Blue Bell is now a bed and breakfast establishment and the Cleveland Arms renamed the Teesdale Hotel.

HUDE (FROM MARKET PLACE) MIDDLETON IN TEESDALE

Middleton – the Hude, a prominence that covers, protects, guards the town from the prevailing winds – a 'hood'. This card was posted on 17th July 1907. On the left in that era was George Pinkney's cafe where he sold confectionery and bakery products. It is now the 'village bakery shop'. Beyond it is an old corn mill overlooking Hudeshope Beck.

Middleton – Seed Hill looking back towards the Market Place. On the right with its oval topped first floor windows is the Mechanics' Institute, Reading Room and Library (Frederick Spraggon, sec.) and next to it the Foresters' Arms where Mrs Nancy Collinson Bell was the publican 100 years ago, though by 1925 the building was a pub no more. The Mechanics' Institute is now the Raby Estates office, and the Foresters Arms – Norman Richardson House – houses the Rural Development Commission. Much of Middleton was developed after the London Lead Company bought an estate in the town in 1815.

Seed Hill. Middleton in Teesdale.

HILL TERRACE, MIDDLETON-IN-TEESDALE.

Middleton – Hill Terrace which is a southward arm of Horsemarket. A pleasant scene showing the substantial houses, trees and village green. The trees have matured in the last 90 years since this postcard was published. This part of the village developed from the 13th century as dwellings spread out from the Market Place and the Hude.

Middleton – looking up Dent Bank on the road out to Newbiggin. Dent Bank, a small hamlet and farm, is about half-a-mile out of Middleton.

Middleton – Schools Holiday Camp. The setting is the old school opened by the London Lead Co in 1861 and closed about 30 years later when a new infants and mixed school opened. The building was then used for dances and other social occasions in the early years of the last century. This postcard was sent on 31st July 1955 to a Mr L. Johnson, Garden Terrace, Leadgate and makes reference to 'cook duty' and 'two troops in the adjacent fields'. It is now an adventure centre, having been previously owned by Sunderland Council.

Middleton – Tees Bridge. This one-arch stone bridge was built in 1811 upon the site of an earlier structure which fell down soon after its construction, burying in its ruins a man and his wife; the former of whom was engaged at the time in pointing out its defects! This postcard was sent from Watgarth Farm, Forest on 30th July 1947 to Joyce in Sunderland and mentions the improved weather and haymaking on Tuesday. Messages haven't really changed over the years.

Middleton – winter in the dales can be difficult, but also picturesque as this scene looking from the Hude towards the Market Place shows.

THE SHOW, GRAIN'S O'BECK.

Grains O'Beck, Lunedale. The 'grains' are the contributary streams, Arngill (and Long Grain Beck) and Lunehead Becks which here unite to form the River Lune. Annual shows were held here in the late 19th and early 20th centuries. Nearby was the Grains O'Beck Inn, run by the Walton family when this picture was taken by D. Sinclair of Middleton in the first decade of the 20th century.

Stanhope Gate Sheep Clipping, No 3, 1913.

Stanhope Gate. Over 10 miles from Stanhope, but overlooking Middleton. Another Sinclair postcard sent from Middleton in 1913 to a Miss L. Sowerby, 109 Church Road, St Anne's on Sea. Sheep clipping was a serious business, but they also hosted social gatherings. Sinclair took a series of photographs, developed them quickly and sold them to attendees at such events.

Stanhope Gate once more, in 1910, showing the ladies at another sheep clipping. Mr Sinclair had an eye for business in terms of the range of pictures he took.

Park End, between Middleton and Holwick. An unknown publisher has lined up young, mature and old for this group picture of the sheep clippers of 1912.

Middleton – Whit Monday sports, with the horse procession which has
attracted a good crowd. This postcard, published by Fred Spraggon of Bridge
studio in the village, dates from about 1909. Mr Spraggon was also the collector
of income tax and operated his studio till at least 1925.

Middleton – Whit Monday sports again, showing the local pierrot troupe. These
minstrels, with whitened faces and loose white clothing, provided
entertainment at, particularly, seaside resorts before and after the First World
War.

Middleton – horse procession again. Another Fred Spraggon card sent on 9th September 1909 from (cousin) Annie at Wythes Hill to Mr W. Swinbank, Clubgill Farm, Coldberry, Middleton – a distance of about 4 miles as the crow flies. The efficiency of the Post Office 100 years ago is exemplorary!

Middleton – there is a serious side to some processions. The 17th Battalion, Durham Light Infantry marching through Middleton. This reserve battalion was formed at Barnard Castle in April 1915. This D. Sinclair published card is one of many issued in the First World War showing servicemen marching through thousands of towns and villages in the land.

Middleton – back to less serious matters. 'Postie' Walton on his round a long time ago!

Middleton School – form 3. Looks modern, but still nearly 40 years ago in 1963. Back, left to right: David Tallentire, Trevor Beadle, Paul Teward, Philip Robinson. Middle: Mr Calder, Melvin Patterson, Jennifer Milner, Jennifer Collinson, Shirley Wilkinson, Keith Jackson, Mr Wilson. Front: Angela Addison, Margaret Stobart, Adele Wearmouth, Gillian Teward, Jean Wearmouth, Kathleen Martin, Sandra Coates, Marion McLoughlin and Rosemary Peirse.

Mickleton – post office. Another D. Sinclair postcard, with the common scene of youngsters posed for the photographer. Teesdale names such as Mickleton, Egglestone and Cotherstone recall Scandinavian settlers in the area. The places would have started as single farms enclosed by wooden stockades and occupied by one family. The current post office is now further down the village – though the original building is called Post Office House.

Mickleton – Quebec Terrace. On the south side of the Middleton-Romaldkirk road. The boys seem to have been interrupted by David Sinclair as they played marbles. These solid stone houses were probably built for the lead miners in the locality.

Mickleton – Bendle Terrace. These houses facing south are on the Low Side part of the village. This postcard was sent from Mickleton to Mrs Dent, 15 Victoria Road, Bridlington on 18th January 1913 and confirms that the writer has arrived safely and will write on Monday.

Mickleton – the chapel in Low Side. It was said at one time that Mickleton was inhabited by Primitive Methodists, Middleton by Wesleyans, Romaldkirk by Church-people, and Cotherstone by Quakers! This chapel is still open today.

Laithkirk Church – about half-mile out of Mickleton is the parish church for Laithkirk, Lune, Mickleton and Holwick. The church was originally consecrated in the 15th century and became a parish church in 1845 when separated from Romaldkirk. It was restored in 1898. From 1864-95 the vicar was W.R. Bell, the antiquary, whose parish magazine contained valuable records of folk-lore and local history. He was found drowned in the Tees in 1895.

Mickleton – Hospital Saturday, 1910. These parades, long before the birth of the National Health Service, were an effective means of financially assisting local hospitals. I wonder what the banner represented? David Sinclair would have known as it is another one of his photographs.

Lunedale – two photographs of the children of Lunedale at school in 1932-33 and 1953. The connection is Miss Roberts who is the teacher shown on both pictures. 1932-33 – standing 4th left is George Addison; sitting, middle 4th left is Gwen Tallentire. 1953, back, left to right: Trevor Dent, Rina Collinson, Donald Jennings, Doris Dent, Paul Addison. Front: ? ?, Heather Dickson, Raymond Robson, Jean Dickson and Stanley Addison.

Blackton Lead Mills, Egglestone.

Eggleston – Blackton lead mills, about one mile north of the village. Lead was first commercially smelted at Egglestone in 1771, and two other mills were later added on as extensions by the London Lead Company. Pack horses were originally used to carry the ore, later supplanted by horse and cart. Eventually, the railway was used from 1867 to bring in coal and take out lead, and the significant amounts of silver which was present in the ore. By 1904 the works had been dismantled, though the premises were still intact in 1925.

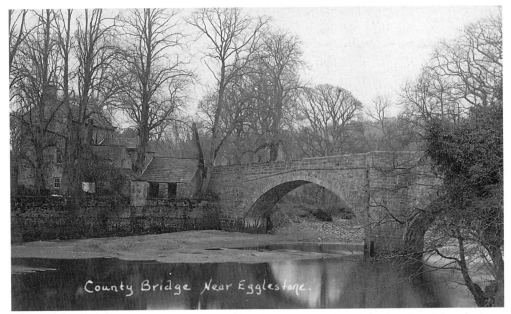

County Bridge Near Egglestone.

Eggleston – County Bridge, connecting Durham on the right bank with what was Yorkshire on the left. There has been a bridge here from the end of the 15th century. It was rebuilt in the 17th. Two lofty, almost pointed, arches thrust boldly into the river upstream and part flood waters like the prow of a ship.

EGGLESTONE.

Eggleston – the only village on the old Durham side of the Tees between Middleton and Barnard Castle. This coloured postcard by Elijah Yeoman, postcard publisher of Barnard Castle, shows the old post office and Three Tuns on the left near the junction of roads to Stanhope, Barnard Castle and Middleton. In 1906 around about the time of this card, William Robert Walker was the sub-postmaster and Thomas Wall the innkeeper. In 1938 Robert Neesham was in the pub and Mary Redfearn at the post office.

Eggleston Hall, once the home of the Hutchinsons, squires, landowners and mineowners, and dates from about 1820. Timothy Hutchinson owned a property here in 1785 at the time of the Enclosure Act, and Cecil William Hutchinson was the owner at about the time of this card in 1906. By 1925 the hall was owned by Sir Willliam Grey, shipbuilder of Hartlepool, and remains the property of the Grey family. The gardens are open to the public.

Eggleston – Institute and School. The school was built in 1820 and Frederick Fawcett was the master in the early years of the last century. The institute was established in 1845 and had a library of 1,000 books. The premises are now the village hall. The spelling of the village name as Egglestone or Eggleston seems to be acceptable in both 19th century and modern publications.

Romaldkirk – with its spacious green set off well in this 1950s postcard. In the middle distance is the Rose and Crown Inn.

Romaldkirk – showing High Green House in Fell Lane. The distinctive canopy is still there today.

Romaldkirk – village stocks and pump. The stocks set with the framework on two boulders. Both stocks and pump are still there today, but the pump seems to have been moved across the village green.

Romaldkirk – St Romald's Church pictured in a modern photograph. Built in the 12th century, the church is cruciform in shape and battlemented. Once the parish was the largest in England, stretching from outside Barnard Castle to Holwick and the far reaches of Lunedale. The parish register includes the details of when the plague came to the North East, in 1644 or 1636 (depending on book sources) when about one third of the people of the parish died, and were buried in mass graves below the village, near the Tees.

Meeting of the Balder and Tees at Cotherstone.

BALDER BRIDGE, COTHERSTONE

Cotherstone – Balder footbridge near the junction with the Tees. This card was published by R. Johnston & Sons of Gateshead, and was sent from Bob at Cotherstone to Mrs R. Renwick, 5 Market Crescent, Philadelphia, Co. Durham on 2nd September 1935. He refers to 'having a really fine time'.

Cotherstone – the swing bridge over the Tees, which looks as though it is really swinging! Unfortunately, not funny. In 1929 too many spectators from a local football match tried to get across the bridge which nearly collapsed with the weight. 25 fell 22 feet into the river, and one – Mrs Sally Nattrass – subsequently died.

Cotherstone – the village with the church of St Cuthbert in the background. The church is quite recent, dating from 1881, and named after the saint whose, legend has it, body rested here before eventually reaching Durham.

Cotherstone – the Red Lion and post office. This card was published by C. & H. Heslop who ran the post office in 1925 when this card was sent from the village to Mr & Mrs Gill, 6 Palm Street, Langley Park. The Red Lion still had its steep thatched roof, which was not replaced until 1935. The post office is now further down the village on the other side of the road.

Cotherstone – west end showing Hagg Gate to the right. The Fox and Hounds Inn is just off the picture, to the left.

Cotherstone – this evocative postcard shows the school boys in military order with their gardening tools, about 1910. The teacher is Mr Ridley, and back first left is Gordon Raine.

Cotherstone – flower show, which had a dance and whist drive as part of the festivities on Easter Monday 1911. The dancers are posed for the photographer.

Cotherstone – the year before, 1910, a hospital demonstration. The audience seem to be listening intently to the speaker, whilst the children in the background play.

Cotherstone School, about 1930. Back row, left to right: Mrs Wight, Fred Clarkson, Stanley Metcalfe, Kathleen Allinson, Phylis Allinson, Greta Watson, ? ?, Elsie Kidd, Betty Hodgson. Third row: Beatrice Bayles, Joyce Thorn, Mabel Thompson, Elsie Robinson, Betty West, Peggy Birkett, Doris Taylor, Nancy Metcalfe, Stan Blenkinsop, George Thorn, Miss Nelson. Second row (kneeling): Roland Swindle, Jack Raine, Harry North, Edith Blenkinsop, Joyce Longstaff, Doreen Bayles, Joyce Carlton, Tom Ridd. Front row (sitting): Blake Kipling, Roland Metcalfe, Geoff Waites, Bill Robinson, Bertha Lowis, John Young, Ernest Thorn, Arthur Thorn, Jack West, Clarence Alderson and Billy North.

Lartington – about one mile from the Tees, through which the Scur Beck flows on its way to that river. Nearby is Lartington Hall built in the reign of Charles I. In a 1937 book, *The Handy Guide – Teesdale* is a saying 'Lartington for Frogs, and Barney Castle for Butchers' Dogs'. The reference was to the very fine fish ponds in Lartington and that the Barnard Castle breed were bull-dogs kept for baiting bulls.

BARNARD CASTLE

Coat of Arms – the postcard firm of Stoddart & Co, Halifax, published coats of arms cards of about 1,000 places in this country. This coat of arms was unofficial in that the town's first official coat of arms was not presented till 1960. The one above is probably the burgesses' seal. This postcard to Mrs Campbell, The Shieling, 24 Churchill Road, Willington-on-Tyne on 23rd August 1944 had a short message – 'Having a nice time. Nice weather. Love, Jean'.

Views of Barnard Castle. Multi-view cards were popular, five for the price of one. Some images, though, were small and indistinct. This Brittain & Wright of Stockton published card of 90 years ago shows the castle, market, bridge, bank and Balgrave's House.

The Sills – actually on the Startforth side of the river, with the black chimney of Ullathorne's mill contrasting with the snow. Also in view is the castle, bridge, river and gasometer! The card is interesting in that it was sent from M.C. in Appleby on 29th July 1905 to Miss E. Peacock, Grains O'Beck, Lunedale. The Peacocks lived at Blake House, just above what is now Selset Reservoir.

A long distance view of the town from the Lendings on the Startforth side of the Tees. St Mary's Church is clearly visible in the middle background. This postcard is only 50 years old having been sent from Olive, 9 Wood Street in the town on 14th November 1951 to Miss Gilhespy, 34 Garron Street, Seaham Harbour.

Another view from the Startforth side, but clearly showing the County Bridge and the jumble of buildings between the Tees and Bridgegate. The tall building near the bridge was Dunn's carpet factory, which was later used by the Salvation Army, and latterly became a games and sporting club.

County Bridge, built and rebuilt on the site of a 14th century bridge over the Tees, formerly connecting the counties of Durham on the right with Yorkshire. Major rebuilding of this bridge took place in 1569 and after the 'great flood' of 1771, plus the addition of smaller arches for added strength in the 19th century. The bridge is open for light traffic only, but is still regularly damaged by manoevering vehicles. This 1939 card also shows the houses, now gone, which extended up to the castle battlements.

A more modern photograph of County Bridge taken in 1973, with Ullathorne's flax mill behind (demolished in 1976) and next to the bridge the house of an 18th century weaver whose dye-kettle in the basement of his house, was submerged in the flood of 1771. The result was cloth of brilliant colour which was in great demand in London. Unfortunately, what the river water had done to his dye-kettle, he was unable to repeat!

This card shows the strategic position of the castle on a 80 foot bluff overlooking a narrow stretch of the River Tees. The castle was founded by Bernard Baliol sometime between 1112 and 1132. His father, Guy, had been granted the lordships of Gainford, Marwood and Middleton-in-Teesdale by William the Conqueror.

A view from the castle of the County Bridge and the (old) Yorkshire side of the river. Note the houses in the foreground this side of the bridge, which huddled themselves beneath the protective buffer of the castle and gave some measure of security in troubled times. The White Swan public house is the first building on the other side of the bridge.

Thorngate Bridge, just below where the Tees abruptly changes direction from south to east. This footbridge was completed in 1884, and was the second one to replace stepping stones which had previously served as a river crossing. On the reverse of this pre-First World War card Edgar writes to Gerty Ablett and says 'this is the old thread mills what you can see of them!'

The new bridge, generally known as the 'water bridge' or Deepdale Aqueduct was built in 1893 to carry water from the Balder and Lune reservoirs to Teesside, but soon became popular as a footbridge which gave new views of the castle and river valley.

Tees Viaduct – 132 feet high and 732 feet long with 5 spans of 120 feet and 2 of 21 feet, was built by the South Durham & Lancashire Union Railway to carry their Stainmore line from Barnard Castle to Tebay and Penrith. The viaduct was built in 1858 at a cost of £20,687, though the whole line did not open till 1861, and closed in 1965 when the only remaining branch to Middleton shut. It was demolished in 1972.

Demesnes Mill – there was a corn mill here from the 12th century situated at the foot of the fields – the Demesnes – owned by the lord of the manor, the Baliols. This postcard shows the natural weir which was instrumental in the siting of the mill. The closed sluice gate can just be seen at the left end of the building by the river. The Demesnes nowadays are freely used for 'exercise and pleasure'.

Horse Market and Market Place from St Mary's Church tower. This postcard was not posted until 1958, but the motor vehicles suggest the photograph was originally taken some years earlier. In the foreground left is the Market Cross.

Horse Market and Market Place in about 1910. The deserted nature of the scene suggests the picture was taken early morning when most good citizens were still in bed. However, the uncluttered scene shows clearly the sweep of the buildings round towards the castle which is behind the buildings on the left.

King's Head Hotel and Market Cross in this 1930s card. A century earlier
Charles Dickens, when researching *Nicholas Nickleby*, stayed at the hotel, and
he gave it a lasting advertisement in the book, by Newman Noggs, speaking of
the inn in the postscript of a letter to Nicholas Nickleby saying: 'There is good
ale at the King's Head. Say you know me and I am sure they will not charge
you for it. You may say Mr Noggs there, for I was a gentleman then; I was
indeed'. The premises have been renamed after the author.

Market Place from ground level. The vehicles suggest a 1950s card. Fifty years
ago traffic was much lighter, though the lack of pedestrians points towards the
photograph being taken comparatively early on a morning.

Two market day scenes – one in the early 1900s and the other over 50 years later. The earlier card was published by Harry Ward who had a stationery and printing business at 21 Horse Market for at least 20 years from 1905 to 1925. The second picture was taken from about the same position as the former and shows few changes in the buildings from one era to the other. The big change is the form of transport from horses and carts to coaches and cars. Both scenes look equally congested.

Market day again. Another early 1900s card, but taken in the opposite direction. The writer has thoughtfully identified the old and new parts of the King's Head. Why? On the immediate right is the Raby Hotel where John Ward was the publican in 1906 and Frederick Woodhams in 1938, whilst Mrs Martha Jane Smith was at the King's Head in 1906 and Fred Dawson 32 years later.

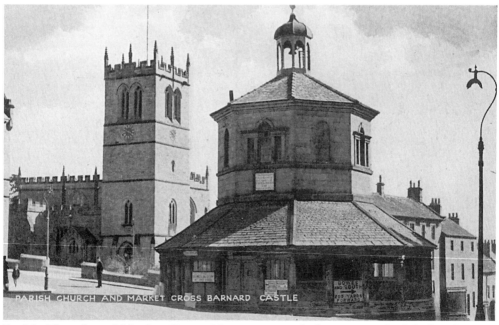

Parish Church and Market Cross. More commonly known as the Market Cross, the Butter Market was built in 1747, a gift of Thomas Breaks. Its function was to provide shelter for farmers' wives who sold dairy produce each Wednesday. It later became a court house, gaol, town hall and fire station.

The Bank from Thorngate. The Bank was once so steep that pedestrians came up and down by a flight of steps, but as it provided the easiest access to the river, it developed as part of medieval Barnard Castle. Today, the oldest part of the town can be seen by viewing the buildings on the Bank and in Thorngate. This postcard was sent on 18th May 1940 to T.C. Eden, Oakmount Boarding School for Boys, Arnside, Westmoreland, and is full of information about what was happening at that time – 'building a great military camp here; putting up great wood huts; all the grammar school lads are joining the new Defence Corps; haven't seen a single soldier yet (at Barney).'

Galgate – formerly Gallowgate and a neighbouring close called Hangslave reminds us that many towns had places of execution, and Barnard Castle's was thought to be here. The straight line of Galgate follows the course of the old Roman road from Bowes to Binchester. The layout shown on this 1950s card was first developed at the end of the 19th century when trees and flower beds were planted. At the bottom of Galgate is the Methodist Church and the area where horse sales and hirings occurred 100 years ago.

Market Day – in Galgate with the cows seemingly wandering at will. The cattle market was held fortnightly on Wednesdays, originally in Galgate, but in 1892 purpose-built accommodation was provided in Flatts Lane. The drinking fountain for people and animals was built in 1873, and it was about that time the process of planting the trees started. The publisher of this card, Edward Albert Metcalfe, had photographic premises at 68 Galgate in the first three decades of the last century. He later moved to 3 Kirk View.

SPRING GROVE BOARDING HOUSE AND NEWGATE, BARNARD CASTLE.

Newgate runs from the Market Cross to Bowes Museum and subsequently on to Whorlton. It is part of medieval Barnard Castle, though the buildings in this postcard represent building in the last two centuries. Spring Grove was the vicarage for St Mary's Church, but was superceded by a new vicarage called the Parsonage in the 1850s. This card shows it after conversion to a boarding house.

St Mary's Parish Church is a battlemented edifice of stone consisting of
chancel, nave, aisles, transepts, north and south porches, and an embattled
western tower with pinnacles containing a clock and eight bells. It was
founded reputedly by Bernard Baliol in the early 12th century, and was
extended and altered in the 14th, 15th and 18th centuries. Some restoration
occurred in 1815, and a total of £6,000 was spent restoring the church in 1870
and building a new tower four years later. Of the original church there remains
only part of the north wall of the chancel with its two widely splayed round-
headed windows. The south doorway dates from about 1170-80.

This Roman Catholic Church was consecrated in 1928, and is sited at the corner of Birch Road and Newgate Street. It replaced St Mary's Catholic Church in Ware Street which was originally built in 1847 as a temperance hall. The bodies of John and Josephine Bowes were re-interred outside the east end of the new church in 1928.

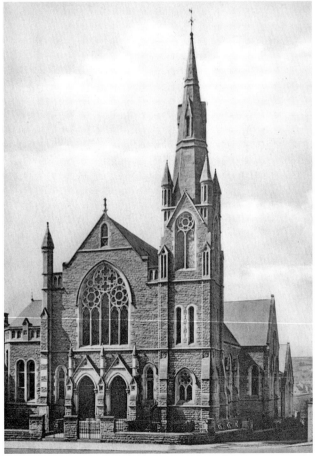

Wesleyan Chapel (Methodist Church) at the foot of Galgate was erected in 1893 at a cost of £5,000; the foundation stone being laid by Lord Barnard in December 1892. The tower is 90 feet high. John Wesley visited Barnard Castle many times between 1752 and 1788; his first meeting being held outdoors on 25th May, 1752.

Primitive Methodist Church, Newgate was erected in 1887 at a cost of £2,124 and could accommodate 350 worshippers. It was closed, and then demolished in 1992. The site is now occupied by flats.

County School. Formerly called the North Eastern County School, it was built between 1883-86 to provide middle class public school education for up to 300 boarders and 50 day boys. In 1924 the school changed its name to Barnard Castle School. This card posted on 3rd August 1958 shows the English Gothic style of the buildings which were built by the same contractor as Bowes Museum, Joseph Kyle. The headmaster in 1906 was the Revd Francis Lloyd Brereton, in 1925 Arthur George Coombs, in 1938 Harold Edward Birkbeck.

Thorngate Mill and (part of) Thorngate Factory. These two modern photographs from 1994 show (above) Thorngate Mill which was the last link with the town's woollen industry, and was still operating into the 1970s producing cloth for the West Riding of Yorkshire woollen industry. It then became a book depository and the intention now is to convert it into flats. Next to the mill is Thorngate Factory which in 1935 was taken over by the North of England Chamois Leather Co as a glove factory and tannery. In 1986 the building was converted into flats.

The Castle – a card published by the Great Northern Railway in their 'Castle Series'. Even though the G.N.R. did not extend north of Shaftholme Junction in South Yorkshire, the company produced postcards of castles at such northern locations as Alnwick, Brancepeth and Raby. There's a short history lesson on the reverse – 'Barnard Castle was built in 1130 and has been the scene of many fierce battles; during the Civil War of Charles I it was captured by Oliver Cromwell after a stern siege.'

View from the castle walls looking up-river with the weir, Water Bridge and Tees Viaduct in receding order in the distance. Dismantling of the castle had occurred by 1637. Some of the stone was used by Sir Henry Vane to expand and strengthen Raby Castle.

Castle – Inner Bayley (or Bailey). This inner court contained all the principal buildings and was separated from the rest of the castle by a moat. On the right is the Keep or Baliol Tower and in the centre the windows of the great hall. Mortham's Tower is on the left.

A view through one of the castle windows. In the distance is the Water Bridge.

Balgroves House, Barnard Castle.
(Where Oliver Cromwell lodged). No. 416

Left: Balgrave's House, Broadgates – named after its 17th century owner. Before that it was an inn; the building probably dating from 16th century. Oliver Cromwell is reputed to have stayed here on the night of 28th October 1648. He was supposedly regaled with burnt wine and shortcakes which fits with its present usage as a restaurant.

Below: Banqueting Hall, Broadgates. This, and the next postcard, were published by Victor Walton of Cromwell House (other name for Balgrave's). In fact he published at least half-a-dozen cards of the premises ranging from the ceilings, cabinet, bedstead and Shakespeare statue inside to the statue of Charles I outside.

BANQUETING HALL, BROADGATES. BARNARD CASTLE

Right: Statue of Charles I, Broadgates. In the 1920s Blagrave's was turned into a museum called the House of Mystery, having antique furniture, armour and instruments of torture, so, presumably this statue of Charles I was part of the museum. Whether Charles ever visited the town, never mind Blagrave's, is not certain, though as Prince of Wales he did own the castle, and certainly visited Sir Henry Vane at Raby in 1633 and 1639.

Below: This statue of Shakespeare was also part of the attractions of the 'House of Mystery'. This was promoted as the only known statue of Shakespeare as a boy, but as Shakespeare was an 'unknown' until he was an adult, how likely is it that a statue would have been made during his childhood? Perhaps more of Mr Walton's flair for publicity!

BROADGATES, BARNARD CASTLE. STATUE OF CHARLES 1

BROADGATES, BARNARD CASTLE
THE ONLY KNOWN STATUE OF SHAKESPEARE AS A YOUTH (BY A. TALATA)

BOWES MUSEUM AND WAR MEMORIAL, BARNARD CASTLE. (14)   88062.

Bowes Museum and War Memorial. In the style of a French chateau, Bowes Museum was built between 1869 and 1875 mostly, but not finally completed and opened until 1892, by which time its benefactor John Bowes and his wife Josephine were dead. The building which cost over £100,000 is 300 feet in length and has an elevation of 85 feet. The central dome is 150 feet high. The museum is now in the care of Durham County Council and contains paintings, furniture, pottery, porcelain and tapestries. It is closely associated with the Strathmore family and the late Queen Mother. The War Memorial in the form of a cross was erected to commemorate the men of the 4th Durham Light Infantry who fell in the Great War, 1914-18.

Right: Bowes Museum – entrance hall. Most of the museum pieces were collected between 1861 and 1875 and represent in its collections every country in Europe of that time.

Bowes Museum – French Furniture Room. The furniture which the Bowes' collected for their chateau in France, at Louveciennes, formed the core of the rooms dedicated to French art. In the background is the Bowes bed which is a piece of ornate carving and gilding with the original curtains and canopy of silk brocade and quilted head panel.

Bowes Museum – the Silver Swan. This is believed to date from 1773, and is a life-size model controlled by three separate clockwork mechanisms. It is still in working order and when operated preens itself and then bends its neck to take a fish from the water.

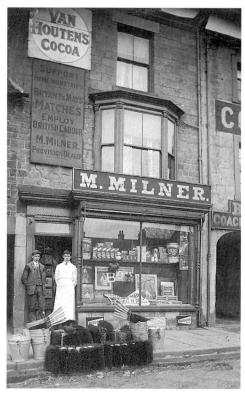

'Surrender or Die.' On the reverse of this card is an abbreviated extract from the *Newcastle Chronicle* – 'A Barnard Castle tradesman was confronted with a blood-curling spectacle on drawing his blind one morning recently. He had erected a new window in his premises without the sanction of the Urban Authority … plans rejected on the grounds that the Council could not give permission for any encroachment on the highway.' Early in the affair some wag trundled this gun from its usual position in Galgate and pointed it at the offending window with a plaque stating the above. In the window is the reply. John George Harris, fish and game dealer, won court actions during 1904-5. His shop was still there in 1925 and run by Will Harris.

Mark Milner's Grocery Shop, 10 Galgate. Note the advertisements for Van Houten's cocoa, Bryant and May's matches, Bovril and Cerebos salt; and the hardware outside – pails, shovels, broom heads. The two men stand posed for the occasion, so was this postcard part of some advertising campaign? Presumably, one of them is Mark Milner. The date of the card is unknown, but probably dates from about 90 years ago. The shop appears in Kelly's Trade Directories of 1906, 1925 and 1938, though by 1938 Mary Jane Milner was in charge.

Peace Process, 1919. There was a procession on 19th July 1919 seen here marching along Horse Market after a church service. The procession included the emergency services, ex–servicemen, choirs and other adult groups, as well as the children's procession seen on the card.

A similar procession to the above, but apparently walking along Bridgegate having crossed the County Bridge, and possibly on their way to the church service.

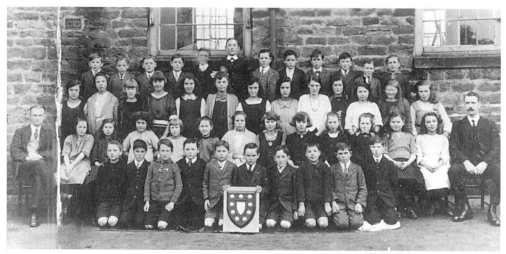

Wesleyan County School, about 1925. Back, left to right: Parkin Jackson
Wallace Bowman, Clifford Franklin, Norman Evans, ? ?, Reg Coates, ? Gill, Jim
Horseman, George Wright, ? Grieveson, Norman Morton, Alan Wright. Third
row: ? ?, Elizabeth Brown, Queenie Coulthard, Enid Lumley, Winnie Huck, ? ?,
? ?, Maude Ascough, ? ?, Nellie Gill, Ena Caygill, Connie Oliver, Emily Stott.
Second row: Mr J.J. Winter, Ethel Ainsworth, Ena Bennett, Annie Ascough,
Edna Turnbull, Madge Rutherford, Doris Rutter, ? ?, ? ?, Maude Rutherford,
Mary Gill, Jessie Swinbank, Mildred Wellman, Mr James Percy Robson. Front:
? Brown, Sid Jones, Trevor Wright, Sid Chaplow, Norman Robinson, Gordon
Kidd, Robert Close, Alan Webster, George Dent and Albert Coulthard. This
school, off Grey Lane, opened in 1830 and had places for 240 pupils.

Beating the Retreat in Galgate, 1954. Do any of the readers recognize
themselves?

Barnard Castle Meet, 1989. The meet, held on Spring Bank Holiday, is still an annual feature with the town band leading a procession of tableaux and old bicyles recalling the origins of the meet – the first annual North-Eastern Cyclists' Meet being held in 1886.

Barnard Castle – from the air. Castle in the foreground, with the Market Place and Horse Market running right to left in the middle background into Galgate running off the photograph back left.

A mildly comic card posted in Barnard Castle on 14th August 1911 and sent to Miss Eva Jordan, 17 Berwick Street, Gateshead, with the message 'How do you like this picture. Love, Jennie'.

This is mile-little game down here.

These milepost postcards were very common. All the publisher did was change the name of each town and they could be identified with any location. Anyway, an appropriate card to turn round and travel away from Barney.

MIDDLE TEES VALLEY

STARTFORTH TO

PIERCEBRIDGE

STARTFORTH CHURCH

Startforth on what was the Yorkshire side of the River Tees. The origin of the name is Streetford, from its position on the Roman road from Lavatrae (Bowes) to Vinovium (Binchester). The Church of the Holy Trinity was built in 1863, replacing an older one of 9th century Saxon origin.

Egglestone Abbey, Barnard Castle. 412.

Eggleston (or Egliston) Abbey was founded probably late in the 12th century by monks of the Premonstatensian Order. About 1195 the Bishop of Durham granted to the abbey the Manor of Eggleston seven miles higher up the Tees. There are only fragments of the cruciform church standing today; parts of the south transept and nave remain, but it is possible to trace the course of the other walls because of site works done by the Ministry of Works.

Barnard Castle, Abbey Bridge

Abbey Bridge, with its embattled walls and one lofty arch, 60 foot high with a span of 75 feet. It was built in 1773 for horse-drawn vehicles. At the south end remains the cicular foundations of a small toll-house. The toll was 1d in 1882 and $1/2$d in 1937. Some things come down in price!

Dairy Bridge over the River Greta, just south of its confluence with the Tees –
the meeting of the waters. Here the dark river dashes through a trench in the
limestone and under an arch of foliage, partly hiding the bridge itself. This
lovely spot has inspired works by Sir Walter Scott, J.M.W. Turner and many
other artists. This postcard is comparatively modern having been sent on 12th
October 1950 from Catterick Camp to Yeovil, Somerset.

Greta Bridge, with its single arch stone balestrudes, was built in 1789 and until
the 1940s carried heavy traffic from Scotch Corner over the Pennines to Penrith.
This card dates from that era having been sent from Norah to Hugh Loftus, 11
Firwood Terrace, Ferryhill on 9th October 1940.

Mortham Tower, Rokeby is a 15th century fortified manor house. The place used to be haunted by the ghost of a Lady Rokeby who was shot nearby by robbers. This 1920s postcard clearly shows the projecting turrets of the tower.

Rokeby Hall, completed in 1731 by Sir Thomas Robinson, is situated on the west bank of the River Greta with Mortham Tower on the east. On the lawn between the hall and the large tree in the right foreground are a group of Roman altars brought, about 1760, from Birdoswald. This postcard dated 15th April 1916 from 'M.B.I.' at Rokeby refers to the hall. Rokeby is the setting for Sir Walter Scott's poem of the same name which he wrote as a visitor to the hall in the years from 1809.

Whorlton Toll Booth. This cast-iron suspension bridge over the Tees has a span of 174 feet and stands 32 feet above the river bed. It was opened on 7th July 1831, replacing a stone bridge which was started on 9th June 1829 and swept away by a great flood on 13th October of the same year. This photograph dating from 100 years ago shows Miss Ann Beadle, the toll collector, outside her toll house on the County Durham side of the river.

A view of Whorlton Bridge from what was the Yorkshire side of the Tees. The toll house can be seen on the extreme left and behind it the steep road up into Whorlton. This bridge is the oldest in the country still suspended on its cast-iron chains. This view dates from between the World Wars, and the card was posted in 1928. Only one light vehicle is allowed on the bridge at a time.

Whorlton Village showing the buildings ranged round the green. In the picture is the local school which opened in 1848 and accommodated up to 110 pupils. The master at the school in 1906 was John Neesom, and in 1925, Charles Edward Edmondson. The school building is now divided into two private cottages, School Cottage and School House. The postcard publisher, George Prudhoe of Darlington, was a stationer at Bondgate in 1906, but by 1925 he was also the agent for the London & North Eastern Railway and a paper and paper bag merchant.

Whorlton Church of St Mary was rebuilt in 1853, replacing an earlier Norman church. The octagonal turret is about 50 feet high and contains two bells. Behind the church is Whorlton Hall. The Headlam family lived in the hall which was occupied by Arthur Cayley Headlam, Bishop of Gloucester, in 1925.

Whorlton – Otter Hunting. Words on the card say: 'Let us join the happy throng, That goes marching along, And we'll all go hunting today'. This card was published by J.H. Skipper of Gainford and sent from Hutton Magna in January 1911 to Miss Hind, c/o Mrs Johnson, 11 Backhouse, Darlington. Skipper tends to be more closely associated with Barnard Castle where he had photographic premises at 42 Galgate.

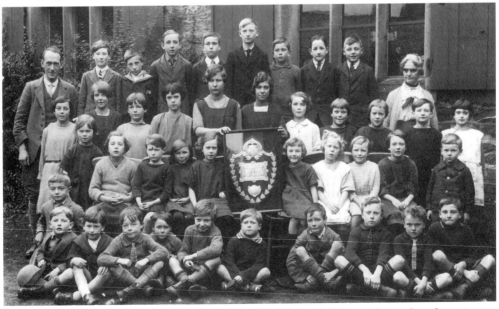

Whorlton School, 1925. Back left is Charles Edward Edmondson, headmaster. Pupils include: Jimmy Alcock, John Alcock, John Preston, Edith Richie, Kathleen Wilson and the Richardsons – Fred, Joe, Robert, Tommy, Watson and Mary.

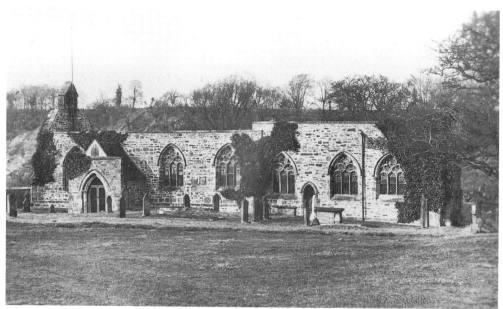

Wycliffe Church with its unusual flat roof. The church of St Mary is mainly 13th century on 8th century foundations, and does not seem to have changed much in 700 years. The church is very near the Tees in a secluded hollow and contains, amongst others, the graves of my great-great-grandparents, William and Margaret Birkett, and their grandson, Birkett Hutchinson. Wycliffe is said to be the birthplace of John Wycliffe, translator of the Bible and reformer of the Established Church in the 7th century.

Wycliffe Hall overlooks the Tees and one of its minor tributaries. Another J.H. Skipper of Barnard Castle postcard. The Manor of Wycliffe was held by the family of the same name until 1611 when, through female heirs, it passed to the Tunstalls and thence to the Chichester-Constable family.

Hutton Magna, also known as Long Villiers – dates from, at least, the Domesday Book of 1086. This postcard from between the Wars shows a number of single storey cottages and the inn on the left, behind the telephone pole. The Oak Tree was let to Mrs Snailham at that time. The entrance to the churchyard is immediately past the inn. On the second right is the Old School House with its small bell tower.

Wycliffe Roman Catholic School, 1952. Hutton Magna has had no school since the 19th century, so children attended here or walked two miles to Whorlton. Back: Morlene Landsdell, Marian Hind, Marie Clark, Joyce Kirtley, Margaret Dobson. Front: Jean Armstrong, Gillian Bennett, Elizabeth Hugill, Pam Fenwick, Doreen Garth and Rosemary Gerheman – in Cinderella (we think).

Hutton Magna – 1953 Coronation Celebrations. The sack race, from left to right: Mr Crusher, Ella Alderson, Catherine Bardon, Nancy Cole, Doris Hind, Rose Tweddle, Jean Ormston, Aline Clark and Doris Smith.

Two churches within half-mile of each other. Top: The parish church of St Mary's at Hutton Magna which was rebuilt from a 13th century chapel, and rededicated in 1878. Bottom: The Roman Catholic Church of St Mary's, Wycliffe, which was consecrated in 1849. Next to it is the presbytery and (closed) school.

Ovington. A.G. Prudhoe of Darlington published the top picture showing the 'Maypole' village which, along with Hutton Magna and Wycliffe, is on the 'old' Yorkshire side of the river. The current maypole is erected behind the trees, left side of road in middle view. The sign at the Four Alls Inn is well known: The Queen: I govern all. A Soldier: I fight for all. A Parson: I pray for all. A Farmer: I pay for all. T. Blackett was the tenant in the 1930s. My great-great-great-great grandfather, Henry Hutchinson, lived in Ovington. Unfortunately, and after 20 years of trying, I still haven't found his father or mother!

Melsonby, Seniors and Juniors, 1950. Children from a wide radius attended this North Riding school 50 years ago. Back, left to right: Nancy Thornton, Madge Cole, ? ?, Nancy Cole, Ray Johnson, Muriel Walker, ? ?, Rosemary ?, Jim Thornton, Pop Martin. Second row: Bob Martin, ? ?, Mavis Waller, Greta Walker, Heather Walker, Lilian Bowman, Jean Layton, Margaret Gregory, Joan Thornton, Pat Hird, Wilf Slater, Tommy Nicholson. Front row: Harry Brown, Keith Waller, Melvin Waller, John Cole, Brian Whitby, Mrs Howitt, ? ?, Elizabeth Brydson, Marina Adams, ? Martin and Marianne Beck.

Winston – the church of St Andrew stands on elevated ground to the east of the village and dates from at least the 13th century. The whole of the south aisle, west end of nave and the tower were rebuilt in 1848. This real photographic postcard was sent on 16th September 1929 from 'Aunty' in Winston to Mrs Keates, 304d Married Quarters, RAF Henlow Camp, Bedfordshire..

Winston – the village in the 1930s. The Manor of Winston originally belonged
to the Nevills, by whom it was granted, in 1313, to the Scropes of Masham. It is
interesting that the village was on the route of a proposed canal in 1770 from
Stockton and Darlington via the pits of South Durham to Winston. That
proposal was abandoned in favour of what later became the Stockton &
Darlington Railway. The petrol station in the picture is now the entrance to a
caravan park.

Winston Bridge, built in 1763-64 from the designs of Sir Thomas Robinson of
Rokeby, is of single span of 112 feet, and was one of the few bridges to survive
the 'great flood' of 1771. The coach parked on the Yorkshire side in this 100
year old picture is said to belong to the Revd Dr Edelston, Vicar of Gainford.

Winston – Mr Gill leading timber at Walker Hall on 29th March 1913. In Kelly's Directory 1906 Mrs Sarah Richardson and sons was farming at Walker Hall. Is the other gentleman Fred who was farming there in 1925 or another son? Postcards of timber leading are quite common during and around the time of the First World War, particularly in Teesdale above Barnard Castle. Walker Hall itself was built in 1777 by a Mr Walker of Cotherstone.

This and the next three cards (*opposite*) show industrial activity in rural south Durham, with boring for coal in 1909 near Winston, and open cast mining in the same area in the 1950s. The bottom two pictures show open cast mining with conventional motive power – a tractor, and with a Sherman tank by a gentleman called Rotinoff near Osmondcroft – sometime after the Second World War.

Selaby Hall, a mile and a bit north east of Winston, was originally a 14th century mansion built by the Brackenbury family. It was substantially rebuilt in the 18th century after earlier alterations in the previous two centuries. Finally, it was modernised and enlarged by Raby Estates. This card was published by J.H. Skipper of Gainford and shows the hall before the First World War.

Gainford – the Ferry. There were two ferries across the Tees here. This one – the commercial one – and a private one. Gainford, whose name derives from Geganford or Gaega's ford, had no bridge and the commercial ferry connected the road running north-south from Ingleton to Eppleby and Forcett. This ferry operated until 1935 and cost 1d, and in Kelly's Directory of 1925, Henry Davison is listed as the ferryman.

Gainford – church and vicarage in a line drawing style in the Teedsdale Series of postcards. The scene dates from the turn of the 20th century though the card was posted during the First World War. In 1971 the oldest part of the village was designated a Conservation Area to secure its protection and improvement. The trees in the foreground are now mature.

Gainford Academy – was housed in these premises from 1819 to 1899. It was possibly better known as Bowman's Academy after the Revd William Bowman the owner. It had 80 boarders in 1864. Its most famous boarder being Arthur Stanley Jefferson (Stan Laurel) who attended the Academy (in other premises in North Terrace) in 1903. An advert in the *Teesdale Mercury* in 1883 lists the school as having five classrooms, cricket pitch, five tennis courts, chemistry laboratory, engineering and surveying classes. The building was given to the village by the Edelston family in 1964, and restored in 1987. Now it houses the Academy Theatre.

Gainford – the Green. County Durham is famous for its green villages, and this one meets the traditional requirements of buildings grouped round a green which was originally used for grazing animals as well as for recreation, sports and other social activities. These houses are in High Row. The young trees in the foreground were planted in 1897 for Queen Victoria's Diamond Jubilee.

Gainford – the Church of St Mary the Virgin dates back to the 13th century and occupies the site of a 9th century structure built by Egred, Bishop of Lindisfarne. The ancient parish of Gainford extended from Piercebridge to Middleton-in-Teesdale, a distance of 21 miles. It was endowed with special liberties, such as the right of execution, goods of felons and other Royal privileges. In 1864-65 the church was restored at a total cost of £3,000. At the date of this card, nearly 100 years ago, the vicar was Charles Henry Watson.

Gainford – the Cross, in the north-west corner of the Green, was erected in commemoration of the 60th anniversary of the accession of Queen Victoria, 20th June 1897, and was unveiled by Lord Barnard on 8th April 1899. It is 12 feet high, and rising from three steps, the topmost of which is the base of an ancient cross formerly existing here. Isaac Charge, local builder, was the stonemason, and the Charge family are still in the building industry today.

Gainford – the Orphanage. On the road east towards Piercebridge, St Peter's Catholic Orphanage Diocesan Certified School for Boys was opened in 1900, and this postcard by J.H. Skipper was probably taken a few years after that. About 140 Basque refugees from the Spanish Civil War stayed here in 1937 for a while until conditions improved back in Spain. It later became an approved school for 45 years until 1984. It is now closed up.

Gainford – road leading to Ingleton, with the houses of West Terrace on the left. Nowadays the building on the right has disappeared. This card was published by J. Norton of Gainford in the early years of the last century, but he does not appear in Kelly's Directories of 1906, 1925 and 1938. Who was he?

Gainford – the Zetland Hunt meeting on the Green opposite the church a 100 years ago. This is a centuries old tradition, but for how long will it last in today's political climate?

Gainford AFC, 1938. Back, left to right: Tommy Ward, Jack Miller, Len Robinson, Mick Phelan, Wilf Oxley, Charles Webb. Middle: Jack Liddle, Arthur Webb, Les Thompson, Jack Middleton, Albert Webb. Front: Jack Chambers, Jimmy Waugh and Kit Hauxwell.

Gainford – Ladies keep-fit in front of the Vicarage in the 1950s. Back, left to right: ? Porterfield, ? Lloyd, Barbara Webb, ? ?, Esther Samuel, Peggy Conway. Middle: Eva Jopling, Alice Liddell, Hannah Graham, Ellen Charge, Ann Allison, Olive Charge. Front: Barbara Donnelly, Margaret Scaife, Janet Pollard, Enid Burdon, Avis Tucker, Muriel Allison and Marjorie Veitch.

Gainford School, 1952. Back row: Mrs Enid Burdon, Robert Webb, Colin
Davison, Edwin Charge, Christopher Charge, Robert Hebdon, John Youds, Joe
Myers, Douglas Allen, Geoffrey Trotman, Mr Claud Cree (headmaster). Middle
row: John Shepherd, Brian Brack, Valerie Hobson, Freda Oliver, Judith Carr,
Barbara Robson, Daphne Brack, Heather Hull, Jean Busby, ? ?, ? ?, Ian Forman.
Front row: Margaret Shaw, Pat Rourke, Flora Dixon, Ann James, Susan Gibson,
Pauline Cairns, ? ?, Prue Johnson, Margaret Robson, ? ?, Christine Forman and
Pamela Harrison.

Fancy dress at Gainford in the 1950s. Included are: Geoff Trotman, Danny Hull,
Freda Oliver, Daphne Brack, John Youds, Margaret Robson, Elsie Oliver, Valerie
Hobson, Edna Elmer, Heather Hull and Jacqueline Trevarro.

Piercebridge – River Tees and Bridge. The present bridge was built in 1673, though it was greatly damaged in the 'great flood' of 1771, and was not rebuilt until 1797 when it was widened on the east side. This Johnston of Gateshead 'Monarch Series' postcard shows the strength of the bridge and the river looking rather calm and benign.

Piercebridge – another Johnston card looking north towards the Wheatsheaf public house (now called Carlbury Arms) at the far end. John Kavanagh was the publican at about the time of this card in the late 1920s. Piercebridge occupies the site of the Roman fort of Magae – which guarded the strategic crossing of the Tees off to the right of this view. In the right block of buildings is the post office which has been run by the Turner family for over 60 years.

Piercebridge – Old George Inn, on what was the Yorkshire side of the river. This Johnston postcard from the early 1930s illustrates the quietness of the roads before the mass invasion of the motor car. Today, you'd be in grave danger taking a photograph from this point. The telegraph poles seem rather intrusive in this shot.

Piercebridge – Old George Inn, now the George Hotel. This card, dating from 100 years ago, has been published before, but it is so interesting that a second helping seems worthwhile. This part of the George was formerly the house next door with the original part of the inn to its right. The portly gentleman right is Robert Lancaster who was licensee at the inn from about 1877 to 1907. Whilst on a walking tour of the district, Henry C. Work saw the old clock in the inn whose story he tells in the one-time popular song, 'My Grandfather's Clock'.

Piercebridge – multi-view, showing the bridge, cottages at end of bridge, north end of village, West View with church bell-tower in background, and Roman remains. The church was built in 1873 and accommodated 150 worshippers.

Carlbury – on the north side of Piercebridge Beck (also known as Dyance Beck). The Railway Inn to the left was run by Mrs Mary Gardner when this postcard was published between the World Wars. The inn was demolished when the Piercebridge by-pass was opened after the Second World War.

Piercebridge School, 1952. Back, left to right: Tony Ratchford, Mick Stephenson, Pat Barrow. Middle: Ann Davie, Glynis Simms, Ann Fothergill, Judith or Margaret Wilson, Joan Holmes, Grace Thornton. Front: Peter Stephenson, Valerie Lord, Valerie Rogerson and Jeffrey Brown.

Piercebridge Silver Jubilee Celebrations, 1977. Back row, left to right, first three partly hidden: Amanda Swanson, Sam Swanson, Michelle Swanson, Jane Holmes, Helen Dodds. Third row: Jeffrey Turner, Susan Stephenson, Simon Stephenson, Michael Joyce, Stephen York. Second row: Donna Joyce, Stephen Shires, Richard Stephenson, Peter Joyce, Elizabeth Dunn, Amanda York, Susan Shires. Front, kneeling/sitting: Craig Massingham, Linda Joyce, Paul Bellas, Mark Weaver, Terry Weaver, Susan Ratchford, Sharon Crooks, Sarah Steel and David Joyce.

STAINDROP, RABY AND INGLETON

Staindrop Primary School Football Team, 1973-74. Back, left to right: Mr Robson (headmaster), Ian Mills, Mark Hedley, Mr Hockey. Second row: Glenn Russell, Rob Davies, David Tarren, Andy Robson, ? ?. Front row: Steve Harman, Keith Hirst, Gordon Nicholson, Michael Wood and Tom Bell.

Main Street, Staindrop

Staindrop – Front Street, which is about half-mile in length and widens out to the west to accommodate the Green, typical of many County Durham villages. Many substantial 18th century stone houses are situated here, so much so that the centre of the village was designated a Conservation Area in 1971 to secure its protection and improvement. Staindrop was one of the seven market towns of the County Palatinate of Durham until 1796 when Barnard Castle became the local market town.

Staindrop – a view in the opposite direction to the above, with the church of St Mary in the distance. On the extreme left edge of the postcard is part of Malvern House, an 18th century red brick house. The pump on the right was erected in 1865 on behalf of Lady Augusta Poulett in memory of Henry, 2nd Duke of Cleveland and his wife, Lady Sophia (Poulett). This postcard dates from 21st September 1915 and is written in code. It was published by M. Copeland. The Copelands ran the post office for at least 32 years, from 1906-1938 according to Kelly's Directories.

Staindrop – Almshouses, situated on the south side, off Office Square. These twelve dwellings and gardens were built in 1862 by Henry, Duke of Cleveland, and 140 years later still look as solid and substantial.

Staindrop – the Green 75 years ago, clearly showing how the village widens out at the west end. The chapel on the left is the Primitive Methodist Chapel built in 1860. The white single-storey building in the left foreground is the former blacksmith's shop. There were two blacksmiths in the village in 1906, Francis Jackson and John Race, and two in 1925 and 1938, Francis Jackson still and Lancelot Wearmouth.

STAINDROP CHURCH.

Staindrop – St Mary's Church – outside and inside. The church, built on the site of an 8th century Saxon church, dates from the 12th to 15th centuries, and was restored in 1849. A significant interest is the memorials to the Nevill and Vane families. The top card was posted in Darlington on 14th September 1907 to Miss M. Cruddas, 26 Archer Sreet, Darlington.

Staindrop – Langley Beck flowing under the Bishop Auckland road. On the left is the southern boundary of Raby Park and round the corner is the South Lodge.

Staindrop – two inns. The Black Swan advertised itself as the cyclists rest. This picture dates from before 1906 as Thomas Robson, who was also a watchmaker, was the licensee then, followed by Clifford Crooks in 1925 and John Thomas Hall in 1938. The Wheatsheaf Inn with a posed group looking steadfastly at the camera. Robert William Blackett was the licensee in 1906, Frederick Stockdale in 1925 and John George Hare in 1938.

Staindrop – 4th Battalion Durham Light Infantry parade in 1912. This battalion was formed in 1853 as the South Durham Regiment and became a regular DLI battalion in 1881. It fought in South Africa in 1902 and in the First World War was a training unit. It was disbanded after the war. The procession is marching down to St Mary's Church. The Georgian Staindrop House is on the left; the residence of Herbert Legard Fife, J.P.

Staindrop – Primitive Methodist Chapel Carol Singers, Christmas 1908. Their chapel was built in 1860 and accommodated 250. They are singing in the grounds of the 16th century Staindrop Hall. The Misses Raine were living at the hall at the time.

Staindrop C. of E. School around 1955. Back, left to right: Trevor Collishaw, Neil Tallentire, Snowdon Young, Billy Scaife, Nigel May, Robin Fell, Neville Singleton, Ian Cotterill, Robin Lily, Dennis Metcalfe, Thomas Hill, Athol Tarn, David Briggs. Middle: David Lee, Jimmy Thompson, Dorothy Gill, Jessica Osborne, Alan Stirk, Lynn Davies, Jennifer Metcalfe, John Osler, Frank Metcalfe, Harry Dale. Front: Julie West, Dorothy Taylor, ? Crampton, Claire Metcalfe, Christine Wardle, Pauline Reed, Olga Leonard, Jean Metcalfe and Pauline Nodding.

Staindrop C. of E. School, Class 1, 1979. Back, left to right: Mrs Stephenson, Matthew Bocock, Mark Cowin, David Robson, Claire Jackson, Leanne Abdale, Zoe Humphries, Warren Reid, Lee Foster. Middle: Sharon Bibby, Elizabeth ? , Paula Milner, Gillian Gill, Ben Johnson, Thomas Whittaker, Alex Cleasby, Miles Thompson. Front: Karen Wheldon, Stephen Clennell, James Bell, Samantha Hewitson, Lee Bell, Daniel Strutt, Sarah Reagan and Sally Waistell.

Raby Cottages – just south of the North Lodge entrance to the castle and its grounds, about one mile north of Staindrop. The nearer cottages were also called Coronation cottages as they were built at the time of the 1902 Coronation of Edward VII. The back cottages are Malt Kiln cottages.

Raby Middle Lodge was situated alongside the A688 road about half-mile north of Staindrop. The low wall, now without its railings, identifies the site today. This picture dates from the 1920s and shows Miss Harker, the lodge-keeper, at her door.

Raby Castle – viewed from the south east, with Joan's Tower far left and Bulmer's Tower nearest right (in shade), and then Chapel Tower and Mount Raskelf far right. Built in the 14th century by the Nevills, most of the castle's interior now dates from 18th and 19th centuries, although its medieval core remains. The Low Pond lies below the battlements in front of the castle.

West front with the Gatehouse far left, Clifford's Tower left, then the Watch Tower and the Nevill Gateway hidden in the shadow of Joan's Tower to the right. Clifford's Tower is 79 feet high, and with walls 13 feet thick, defended the Gatehouse.

Four interior views published by Photoway of Fleet Street Ltd. My estimate is that there were at least nine in the series, dating from 50-60 years ago.

Entrance Hall – part of the original medieval structure, was created in its present form in 1787 to celebrate the coming of age of the 2nd Earl of Darlington. Carriages could drive right through the hall from the outside into the Courtyard, left to right in this view.

Barons' Hall – considerably changed from its structure in 1579 when 700 knights met to plot the Rising of the North against Elizabeth I. The floor level was raised 10 foot when the carriageway underneath was constructed. The hall was extended by over 50 feet over the Octagon Drawing Room, and the roof replaced by a more elaborate one. At the far end the 600 year old Minstrels' Gallery was significantly altered in 1864 when the doorway at the far end, to the Grand Staircase, was inserted. The portraits in the hall are of the Vane family who bought the castle in 1626 from the Crown and who still own it today, in the person of the 11th Lord Barnard.

Right: The Chapel – the medieval chapel which dates from 1364-67, was once separate from the rest of the castle, but was substantially restored in 1848 in relation to the floor, window traceries, roof and wall finishings. In 1901 more restoration occurred in respect of arcade, decor, pew ends and windows.

Below: The Library – originally one long medieval room, it was divided into two rooms by Sir Henry Vane in the early 17th century, and was further altered in 1870. It was once a dining room and is now a drawing room – which is reflected by the furnishings on this card. 'Staindrop from her sylvan bowers, Salutes proud Raby's battled towers.' (Rokeby). The castle and grounds are well worth a visit.

A DANCE

Will be held in the

SCARTH MEMORIAL HALL,

STAINDROP

On SATURDAY NOVEMBER 13th, 1909.

DANCING TO COMMENCE AT 7-30.

Proceeds for the Funds of the Staindrop Quadrille Band.

Admission :— Ladies 6d. Gents 6d.

Music will be supplied by Members of the above Band.

Preston's Excelsior Printery Staindrop.

Two contrasting social advertisements. The Scarth Memorial Hall was built in 1874-75 as a testimony to T.F. Scarth, estate agent to the 4th (and last) Duke of Cleveland. Note the entrance price of 6d in 1909. Barforth Hall, Gainford which hosted Acker Bilk, is on the (old) Yorkshire side of the Tees, but connected to Gainford by a minor bridge. This bridge, at the time of my visit in July 2002, is structurally unsafe but still seems to be in use by the occasional pedestrian.

STRANGER ON THE SHORE

BARFORTH HALL GAINFORD **30'-**

By invitation of Mrs. Graham

FRIDAY 31st JULY 1964 9pm to 2am

DANCING TO **MR. ACKER BILK'S**

Paramount Jazz Band with THE CONCORDES

SUPPER INCLUDED IN THE PRICE OF ADMISSION

LICENSED BAR · TOMBOLA · SEA FOOD & CHAMPAGNE BAR

Ingleton – Front Street from the north side in this postcard published by
G. Prudhoe, Darlington. The village was supposedly a small farming
community inhabited from Saxon times and, until 1845, part of Staindrop
parish. This postcard dates from the 1950s and was sent from Maggie to Mrs
Atkinson, Wynhurst, Durham Road, Wingate on 22nd August 1955. It was
posted in Gainford, but makes reference to Ingleton. In the shadow is St John's
Church.

Ingleton – West End. A Lilywhite of Halifax card from the 1930s. On the right,
with the petrol pumps, the premises of Herbert Bowles, cycle dealer, boot dealer
& draper, and petrol station.

Ingleton – Wheatsheaf Inn at the eastern end of the village at the junction with the Gainford Road. Originally the village had four public houses, though by 1906 that had reduced to two.

Ingleton – horses at the Wheatsheaf Inn nearly 100 years ago when George William Howe was the landlord. Jacob Dunn was in charge in 1925. It was a blacksmith's in the 1960s, and is now a private house undergoing renovation.

Ingleton – Black Horse Inn. This is the only public house left in the village. This postcard dates from before the First World War. The publican in 1906 was William Burney, in 1925 Thomas William Bowman and Vasey Thompson in 1938. The building to the left of the pub is no longer there.

Ingleton School – a view from the 1930s. The school opened in 1819 according to Kelly's Directory, and was enlarged in 1874 and 1893 to accommodate 164 children. Albert A. Wade was the headmaster from 1915-48. This school closed in 1967 when the present one in Manor Road opened. The sundial shown on this Lilywhite of Halifax card was incorporated in the south wall of the new building.

Ingleton School, 1930. The long serving headmaster, Albert A. Wade, is on the right and Miss Bee on left. Pupils included: Herbert Allison, Ethel Bainbridge, John Bainbridge, Gordon Bayles, Laurence Binks, Tommy Bowles, Harry Brown, Herbert Crooks, Herbert Dawson, Geoff Dent, Muriel Dodds, Reginald Forster, Ada Gibson, Arty Harland, Ivy Harland, Ethel Heslop, Sid Hodgson, Mary Horner, Geoff Knibbs, Ethel Parkin, Eddie Pinkney, Alice Ruddick, George Scurr, Ernest Snaith, George Snaith, Mary Spence, Esmond Stobbs, Jenny Thompson, Joseph Todd, Greta Townson, John Wade, ? Atkinson, ? Bradbury and ? Parkin.

Ingleton School, 2001. Back row, left to right: Mrs Ray, Christopher Parker, Peter Forster, Rebecca Toms, Michael Armstrong, Philip ? , William Forster, Mrs Bainbridge. Third row: Sarah Stephenson, Sally Robinson, Matthew Fearnyhough, Andrew Fearnyhough, Freya Clarke, Tilly Lanigan. Second row: Joseph Hodgson, Jessica Hunter, Millie Peart, Thomas Brown, Emily Campbell, Oliver Pearce, Amber ? . Front row: Pippa ? , Jenny Stephenson, Lucinda Elliott, Edmund Clarke, Rebecca Westgarth and Alicia Armstrong.

Keverton Clog Works. This picture from 1932 shows the workers posed in front of a supply of tree trunks. Back, left to right: Charlie Raison, Tom Caygill, Harold Patey, John Bailey, Ernest Nodding, Denis Cody. Third row: Harry Walker, George Metcalfe, Bill Lightfoot, Willie Woolf, Joe Robinson, Max Foreman, Dick Race, Arthur Thompson. Second row: Harry Grice, Tom Scanlon, Nelson Lowson, Jim Hardy, James Maude, Tom Pearson, Jim Hayhurst, John Hayhurst, Willie Hodgson. Front: Ron Sutcliffe, Jack Caygill, Fred Lightfoot, Ronnie Bird, Eddie Tarn and John Cody. Little boy – Pat Cody.

The works, at the top of Keverstone Bank off Burnt House Lane, was one of the last clog factories in the North East. This mill, which was an off-shoot of a firm which had been in the clog sole business for over 100 years, opened in 1921. At that time 32 men were employed to fulfil the large demand for clogs from the mill workers of Lancashire and Yorkshire. The clogs were made by cutting tree trunks down their full length. The planks were then cut into lengths according to the size of the clogs and shaped from patterns on several different saws. Steaming at 90lbs pressure drew the sap out of the wood which was then left to dry naturally. In 1929, 700-800 dozen pairs of clogs were produced each week, falling to 200 dozen in 1972. In that year productivity was gradually run down with the workers leaving in batches of five or six at a time, until on 31st May the factory closed after 50 years of turning beech and sycamore trees into traditional wavy-soled clogs. By the summer of 1972 two people were still employed – taking down the mill. It's ironic in that the early 1970s was the era of fashion wooden-soled clogs.

Streatlam Castle – two views of the castle which was the seat of the Bowes family from the 14th century when Adam Bowes became lord of the manor by marrying Alice Trayne. The ownership of Streatlam descended with the Bowes family till 1767 when Mary Eleanor Bowes married the 9th Earl of Strathmore – the Lyon family. The castle remained with the Bowes-Lyons – apart from John Bowes' (of Museum fame) tenure from 1820-55, until the 1920s when it was sold to Norman Field. Later the castle was partly demolished with the intention of revealing its 15th century core. However, the shell of the castle eventually became unsafe and in 1959 was blown up by the Territorial Army during a field exercise. A sad end to a country house visited regularly by the late Queen Mother when her brother lived there early in the last century.

THE RAILWAY
DARLINGTON–BARNARD CASTLE– MIDDLETON-IN-TEESDALE

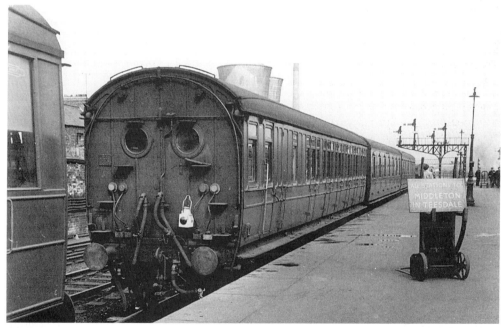

Darlington Bank Top station – the terminus for trains from Barnard Castle and Middleton. This 1956 view of platform 5 showing the information board perched on the upturned barrow, and the 'push & pull' carriage set on the left. The line to Barnard Castle opened on 8th July 1856 nearly 24 years after prominent Barnard Castle business men first agreed that they wished to see an extension of the Stockton & Darlington Railway to their town. The chief opposition had come from the 1st Duke of Cleveland and his son who did not wish a horrid railway through the beautiful Vale of the Tees. After years of negotiation, the 2nd Duke eventually indicated that he would remain neutral about the railway if the line avoided Selaby Park. So, on 3rd July 1854 the Parliamentary Bill in respect of the line became law.

Piercebridge Station was the first station after Darlington North Road. This postcard view dates from approximately 1908, and everyone, including the signalman, is posed for the camera. John Gedling was the stationmaster at that time and is probably the gentleman in the bowler hat.

The same station nearly 50 years later, with very little change. The train headed by a class J21 locomotive of North Eastern Railway vintage is heading for Darlington about five miles away. Tom Cooper was in charge at Piercebridge from 1945-64.

Francis R. Wrightson (*inset photo*), born in 1840, was the stationmaster at Piercebridge from 1875 until his untimely death in 1901. The main photograph dates from 1889 and shows Francis, his wife Eleanor and daughter.

Piercebridge – class K2 locomotive no. 62048 propelling a brake van through the station on 28th August 1965. Ray Goad of Darlington travelled the line extensively in its last few weeks taking many photographs as a permanent record of the last days. This is one and more appear later.

Forcett Branch opened in 1866 and ran from a junction two miles west of Piercebridge for five miles to Forcett where it served local limestone quarries. This is the terminus not long before closure on 2nd May 1966. Some agricultural goods were also handled, but the line existed for the quarry traffic which was as high as 1,280 tons per day in the 1880s.

Gainford Station. This is a postcard from the early 20th century looking east towards Piercebridge, over two miles away. Again the station staff are posed for the photographer. Gainford was the only station between Darlington and Barnard Castle which was effectively in the village, so as to avoid the Selaby Park estate of the 2nd Duke of Cleveland. Richard Humphrey was the stationmaster when this postcard was taken.

Gainford Station about 50 years later, but the view is in the opposite direction. The station house is still there today set in the midst of much later housing development, but it has its old Stockton & Darlington Railway numbered plaque on the wall. Note how well rural railway stations were kept in the decades until the 1960s.

Gainford – station and station house on 26th February 1965, six weeks before closure of the line west of Forcett Junction.

Gainford – one of the two bridges over the Tees west of the village built to avoid the Selaby estate. Class G5 North Eastern Railway locomotive pulling a passenger train towards Barnard Castle. These two bridges were the only major engineering works between Darlington and Barnard Castle as the railway ran through open undulating country.

On 24th October 1905 at Grant Cottage, west of Gainford, two locomotives pulling a goods train were derailed because plate-layers had mistakenly removed a rail. Fortunately, injuries were minor. However, the mishap generated great interest from the general public in respect of the incident itself and the recovery of the locomotives, numbers 1135 and 1219, and the wagons. Locomotive no. 1219 of Stockton & Darlington Railway design had been built in September 1869 at North Road Works, Darlington. It was scrapped in 1909. The other locomotive no. 1135 of North Eastern Railway design had been built at Gateshead Works in the 1850. The first of the three cards was sent from G.L. to Mr T. Bates, stationmaster, St John's Chapel, Weardale on 31st October. Unfortunately, the local publisher is unknown.

Number 1135 is nearest the camera, with no. 1219 half-way down the embankment.

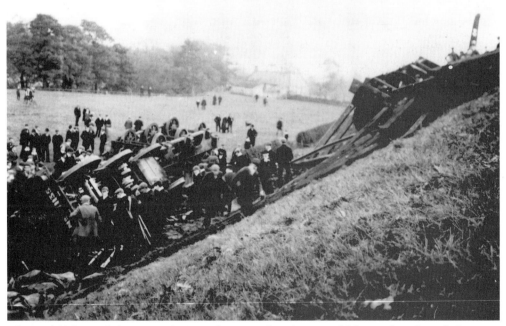

The publisher of these cards is unknown, but he would have developed the photographs quickly, and be selling postcards to onlookers before the wreckage had been cleared away. At least half-a-dozen different views have been traced.

Winston Station – looking from the foot bridge west in the early 1900s; goods shed on left, station house to right. The view looks as though two pictures have been put side-by-side.

Winston – looking to the east in the early 1900s. Notice the station sign 'Winston for Staindrop' – being two miles away and never served directly by rail. Walter Willson's and Bovril advertised on enamel signs on the right. The stationmaster would be David Young about that era. Is that him on the left?

Winston on 26th February 1965. The platforms were staggered each side of the level crossing. The station area is now a transport depot.

Westholme Sinkers, 1911. Railway industrial traffic included coal and stone. The only commercial coal mining in the middle Tees Valley took place in the Winston area. The original Westholme Colliery operated before the First World War, though had closed by 1914 to be replaced by the new Westholme Pit nearby bored by the Hetton Colliery Company. It was soon abandoned because of gas, flooding and geological problems. The nearby village of South Cleatlam was built to house the miners. In addition, Kelly's Directory of 1906 includes an entry for Bell & Lawson as proprietors at Osmondcroft and Whorley Hill Colliery – which also included Newsham Drift. In more modern times, North Tees Colliery, near the main Darlington road west of Winston, was operated by J.W. Johnson from at least 1928. It was closed by the National Coal Board in 1965. A small colliery opened at Osmondcroft in 1988, but is now closed.

Newsham Rail Sidings, 1910. Stone from Dunhouse Quarry being loaded from horse-drawn vehicles into the railway wagons.

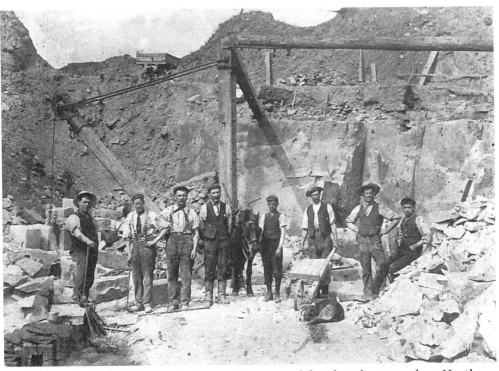

Dunhouse Quarry, 1905, with the workers posed for the photographer. Hartley Bros ran this and other quarries at Cleatlam, Darlington and Stainton at this time. Jennison & Turnbull were quarrying here in 1925.

Broomielaw Station, one mile south of Streatlam Castle, was originally a private station used only by people employed by the estate and receiving mail. However, it was very busy during and after the Second World War when the area housed thousands of soldiers at Stainton, Streatlam, Westwick, Barford, Humbledon and Deerbolt camps. The station was also used by the late Queen Mother when she visited her brother who lived at the castle from 1905 to 1914. Broomielaw Private Station as it was listed in Kelly's Trade Directories of 1906 and 1925, had a station porter only – Charles Porter in 1906 and George Elliott in 1925. The top photograph shows Broomielaw in 1959 when redundant locomotives, such as class A8 no. 69831, were stored on the old coal drop sidings. The lower photo shows the station, looking east, on 28th March 1965, the year of the line's closure.

The next few photographs show the rail facilities at Barnard Castle over the 109 years to closure in 1965.

Above: The first station at Barnard Castle opened in 1856. It was a terminus station behind Galgate, but only lasted as a passenger station until 1861 when the through station on the Stainmore line opened. The original then became a goods station.

Above: Barnard Castle second station after closure in 1965. It was constructed from yellow sandstone in cottage style. The expansion of the GlaxoSmithKline premises have obliterated most of the railway relics in the town.

Right: Percy Wrightson, grandson of Francis the old stationmaster at Piercebridge, was stationmaster at Barnard Castle from 1940 until 1952. In 1906 the stationmaster was Tom Cooper, grandfather of the last stationmaster at Piercebridge, also called Tom. Cornelius Leigh was in charge in 1925. Railway employment was a family business in many instances.

Mr Wrightson remembered the 1947 winter when railway communications with the west were cut off for weeks. This scene from the signal box shows the station in that dreadful winter.

Barnard Castle on 24th July 1957. Class G5 no. 67258 is about to couple up to a train for Bishop Auckland. The train started at Middleton, but the locomotive was detached at Barney to take on water. The station consisted of a long single through platform, partly covered by an overall roof, with a bay at each end. To the left were loops and sidings for handling the Stainmore traffic.

Barnard Castle in about 1960. The tracks to the east bay platform have been removed and diesel railcars have replaced steam.

Rail tours were common as the age of steam and branch lines drew to a close. On 25th April 1964 class V3 no. 67637 and class 4MT 42639 on the Railway Correspondence & Travel Society 'The North Yorkshireman' leaves the west end of Barnard Castle for Middleton.

Above: Lartington Station was the first station west of Barnard Castle on the South Durham & Lancashire Union Railway, and was opened in 1861 at the same time as the railway between Barnard Castle and Tebay, Westmoreland. This postcard from about 1910 shows the substantial station house. The station sited at the north end of a cutting, closed on 22nd January 1962 when the Stainmore line shut.

Right: Members of the Northumberland Hussars detraining at Lartington, possibly on their way to Deerbolt Camp. The band are getting ready to play in this postcard from about 1915.

Cotherstone – a postcard from the early 1900s of the branch railway which opened on 12th May 1868 and ran for nine miles from Tees Valley Junction to Middleton-in-Teesdale.

Cotherstone about 1960 when diesel rail cars had taken over passenger duties. The station was of single platform with the single-storey facilities grouped at the village end of the platform. In the distance to the right some of the village houses can be glimpsed.

Romaldkirk – a postcard again from the 1900s, showing the single platform and simple building. This branch was intended to be part of a line from Barnard Castle to Alston, but it was not possible to raise the necessary amount of capital in 1871.

Romaldkirk, on 27th July 1957 class A8 no. 69863 heading into the station on its way to Sunderland via Barnard Castle, Bishop Auckland and Durham with the 5.53 pm from Middleton-in-Teesdale. Ian S. Carr, the photographer, then boarded the train here to take him back to his home in Sunderland.

Mickleton – two miles from Middleton; another quiet country station, with buildings not as substantial as those at Romaldkirk. A postcard sent in 1914 from niece Mabel, East End, Mickleton to Mrs W. Swinbank, High Skears, Middleton.

Mickleton in much later days. A photograph taken in the 1950s with locomotive class A8 no. 69834 at the head of a train bound for Middleton. Note how unkept the station had become.

Middleton-in-Teesdale. The terminus had more commodious facilities for passengers, but a single platform was still sufficient for the passenger traffic. The station being half-a-mile from the village did not help to generate customers. The upper card shows the station in about 1910. Note the horticultural exhibits on the middle card, which were quite typical of rural stations. The stationmaster around this time was William Collin, with Lancelot Forster there in 1925. The lower view is from the mid 1950s with a class A8 locomotive setting off on its journey down to Barnard Castle. There was significant stone traffic at Middleton. A line ran for two miles to Ord & Maddison's Crossthwaite whinstone quarry as well as much shorter sidings serving the firm's Middleton quarries. Middleton closed to passengers on 30th November 1964, and to goods on 5th April 1965. Most of the site is now a caravan park.

Some views of the post-railway era in the Tees Valley.

Lune bridge above Mickleton, 1994.

Gainford bridge over the Tees, 1994.

Lartington station – now a private house,
1994.

Broomielaw Station, 1993.

Some views of the transport competition.

Right: Sam Turner of Barningham, 1922. Front vehicle: Ford Model T, reg. AJ945, 14-seater. This vehicle carried passengers to markets at Darlington, Barnard Castle and Richmond on Monday, Thursday and Saturday respectively, and was used to deliver coal on other days! Rear vehicle: Ford 4-seater, registered 12th July 1919, reg. U448.

Left: Chevrolet, HN3396, 14-seater, as new, in Gainford in 1924. The Darlington Triumph Services were developed by David Todd with over 50 buses and were a household name in Teesdale in the period 1923-50.

Right: Bedford, UP5850, 20-seater of 1931 vintage, in about 1948-49. The location isn't certain, but somewhere above High Force seems likely. Teesdale Queen, was a company owned by a Mr Bainbridge, which was eventually acquired by Joseph Wilson, formerly of the Fawn Lea Omnibus Co.

In June of Golden Jubilee year, 2002, Avis Charge (now Mrs Tucker) and Joyce Allan (now Mrs Line) recreate the cover photograph of their 1937 scene. Many thanks to them.

The People's History

To receive a catalogue of our latest titles send a large SAE to:

The People's History
Suite 1
Byron House
Seaham Grange Business Park
Seaham
County Durham
SR7 0PY

www.thepeopleshistory.co.uk